Collins Educational

First published in 1989 by William Collins Pty Ltd
Sydney, Australia

First published in 1991 in Great Britain
by Collins Educational
London and Glasgow
A HarperCollins company

Text copyright © Nigel Croser 1989

The author asserts the moral right
to be identified as the author
of this work.

Illustrations copyright © George Aldridge 1989

Copyright Book Bus edition
© Collins Educational 1991

Book Bus editor Pat Green
All rights reserved
No part of this publication may be reproduced
or transmitted by any means without the
permission of the copyright owner.

ISBN 0 00 313659 0

Typeset by Adelaide Phototype Bureau Pty Ltd.
Printed and bound in Hong Kong.

HELP!

Nigel Croser
Illustrated by
George Aldridge

Collins Educational

For Jo

'What a ride,' gasped Elephant.

'That storm came from nowhere,' said Lion.

'Fishing one minute, shipwrecked the next!' said Monkey. 'Now what shall we do?'

'I wonder . . .' thought Beaver.

Elephant took charge.

She would save them.

'I am the biggest,
so I am the boss,' she said.
'And I have a plan.'

She climbed upon the rocks
and squirted a fountain of water
high into the air.

'This will bring help,' she shouted. 'Someone in a boat or plane will see me and we'll all be saved.'

So Lion and Monkey
sat on the beach and watched
as Elephant squirted and waved
as hard as she could.

But Beaver was doing
what she liked doing best –
chopping down trees with her big
front teeth.

Elephant squirted and waved
and waved and squirted all afternoon.
By evening she was so tired that
her water fountain was just a little dribble
and she couldn't wave at all.

Two boats and three planes had passed by
the island,
but no one on board had seen her.

'We've wasted a day,' said Lion.
'I am the King of the Jungle
and I have a plan.
Tomorrow you'll do what I say.'

When Lion woke up next morning,
Beaver was already doing
what she liked doing best –
chopping down trees with her big front teeth.

Elephant was snoring loudly,
and Monkey was pretending to sleep.

'Wake up! Wake up!' roared Lion.
'It's castle-building time.'

Beaver came when they called her.
'Here!' cried Lion.
'There!' cried Lion.
'Faster!' cried Lion as he made them all work.

By lunchtime they had built
the tallest and most wonderful sandcastle
in the world.

Lion climbed to the very top and there he sat,
with his head in the air, looking very, very important.

'Someone will see me and we'll all be saved,' he said.

Just then a breeze began to blow across the island, tossing sand from the castle into the air.

Lion looked a little worried
and not quite so important
as the breeze grew stronger and stronger.
Before long the wind was howling
and the sandcastle was blowing away.

Lion roared and waved
when a plane flew over the island,
but the pilot did not see him.

That night Monkey could not sleep.

'I have a plan,' he said
and he clapped his hands with excitement.
'How good it feels to be clever.'

When Monkey woke up the next morning, Beaver was already doing what she liked doing best – chopping down trees with her big front teeth.

But Lion was snoring loudly, and Elephant was pretending to sleep.

'Lazy lumps,' said Monkey.
'And anyway, I'm so clever I'll do it myself!'

'I'm building a bonfire,' he shouted.
He began to gather twigs and branches.

Beaver ran when she heard him call
and quickly brought him more wood.

'It's ready to light,' cried Monkey at last and everyone gathered to watch. 'Someone will see the smoke and we'll all be saved.'

But then it started to rain.

The first drop landed on Monkey's nose.
He looked a little surprised and not quite so clever.
The second drop made a loud, hissing sound
when it splashed into the fire
and the next few did the same.

Then the rain poured out of the clouds,
put the fire out, and washed it away.

As a plane flew over the island,
Monkey blew desperately upon the ashes.
There was only a wisp of smoke
and the plane soon disappeared.

Beaver hurried away.
Soon she was doing
what she liked doing best –
chopping down trees with her big front teeth.

Elephant, Lion and Monkey sat down.
They looked very, very worried.
'We're finished,' said Lion.
'There's nothing left to try,' said Elephant.
'Even I can't think of anything,' said Monkey.

All day long they sat there. All day long they moaned.
Suddenly they heard another plane.

Elephant ran to the water.
She waved her trunk and
squirted a fountain high into the air.
Lion stood tall on a mound of sand
and Monkey blew on the ashes
to make them smoke again.

But Beaver kept doing
what she liked doing best –
chopping down trees with her big front teeth.

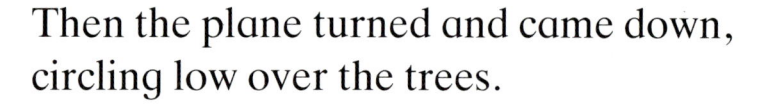

Then the plane turned and came down,
circling low over the trees.

'They've seen me!' cried Elephant.
'They're coming.'

'They've seen *me*!' cried Lion.
'They're waving.'

'They've seen **me**!' cried Monkey.
'They'll soon send someone to take
us all home.'

At the edge of the trees stood Beaver.
She was tired. Very tired.

She looked up as the circling plane came near.

The pilot was smiling . . .

Beaver was smiling too.